Dear One

poetry by
Eryn Talcovsky

Talcovsky Independent Press

CHAPTERS

dedicated to my lord and
savior Jesus Christ, without
whom i would be hopeless.

Chapter One

Dear One

we met up again
all those years later
and you asked me
if i remembered you

what a ridiculous question.

how could i have once
loved someone
so deeply
and ever forget them?

you taught me
to step into life
embracing its risks
living freely

i found myself gazing
out the window
looking out at the snow
watching it fall

but as always
my thoughts
drift towards you

i just can't seem
to keep you
off my mind

take care of your heart
caress it tenderly
and show it love

i have spent so much time
searching
that i don't know
if i would recognize
what i'm looking for
if i found it

when i look into his eyes
all i can see
is the memory

of the time we were alone
in the mountains
around a campfire
and i looked so deeply
into your eyes
and forged such an iron bond
between our souls
that the image of your irises
is seared into my mind

when i look into his eyes
all i can see
is a shadow
of what i had
with you

we are put here on this earth
to grow
and find
our joy

i was playing my guitar
and he was singing
and i swear the music we made
in that moment of connection
could have changed
the whole world

all at once it felt

safe, yet dangerous
normal, yet risky
loving, yet lustful
pure, yet dirty

the first time
our lips
touched

does she love you
like i loved you?

no, she doesn't
because nobody ever could.

for a split second
i thought
that i recognized you
in the wax-mart on 5th street

my heart fluttered
and i wondered how i might
make it look
as if we
bumped into each other
on accident

but excitement turned to
disappointment
for it wasn't you

it was merely a mirage
in the desert
the illusion of water
playing tricks on my desperate
thirst
to be reunited with you
once more

surround yourself
with the beautiful
in life

let it flow through you
and connect you
with yourself

you remind me
of a warm cup of tea
on a rainy Tuesday afternoon
back in london

oh, the rules i would break
for you
if only i got a taste
of what we once had
in return

he looked at me
in that moment
as if i was the only thing
worth his attention
in the entire world

dear god
let me be with
the one i love
for all eternity

grant me this, i pray
so that my heart
may at last rest
and cease its endless aching

everything felt different
with you

kiss me.

kiss me like your life
depends on it
kiss me like the world
is about the end
kiss me like our love
is insatiable

i don't care, just kiss me;
that would be enough.

i find myself writing for you
and only you
hoping you'll pick up this
book
and find in it
pieces of yourself
for everything, it seems
goes back to you

maybe i'm sick
infected with the idea
that we could love each other
the way we do in my dreams

be grateful for the friends
in your life
who stay by your side
through thick and thin
and pull you back
when you go too far

take me to the depths
of your deepest feelings

be the tour guide
of your own pain

teach me to trace my fingers
along the scars
that permeate your soul

take me to the depths, dear
one
take me all the way.

what magic it is
to be loved by someone
who could have anyone
but still chooses
you

to be an artist
means being someone
who cannot help
but create

i am cursed by the longing
to fix you

to shorten the time
between your texts
and make you see
why i'm right for you

i wish you could see
how happy we could be..

if i could take all
of your pain
and all
of your brokenness
and bear your burdens
myself

i would do it
in a heartbeat

<u>Chapter Two</u>

Hope

he may have broken you
but your inner light
is far stronger
than anything
he could ever do to you

your limitations
are only constructs
of your own mind

you are powerful indeed
and capable of so much more
than you
could ever know

though it may not feel
like it right now
you have a future
and you will go
far beyond
where you are right now

nothing can truly hurt you
as long as you have
hope.

to gaze at life
and see it
for all of its beauty
is a wonderful thing

it feels like a glass
of cold water
for the soul
on a hot summer day

the strongest bonds
are with those
who you've been through
things with

the people who
are the shield to your sword
and have your back
through everything

i used to try
to cover up
my freckles
because i was made fun of
in grade school

but you looked at them
with a loving gaze
and told me
i was beautiful
and now
i look in the mirror
and see beauty
where i used to see
pain

if you really care
about someone
pray for them
in the morning

growing pains
may hurt now
but they signal
the coming
of brighter days

so take heart
as you go
through the tunnel

take heart
for the light
will always come.

never forget
where you came from.

do not forget
that a flower needs roots
to keep it from
blowing away
in the wind

and you need roots
to hold you down
when things get hard

so again, i say
never forget
where you come from.

you are my strength
when i am weak
you are my shield
when arrows fly
you are my hope
when all is dark
and you are my god
who will never let me go

be careful
not to spend
too much time
looking at your feet
trying not to stumble
when you are weary

remember to look up
at the stars
and remember your hopes
remember that there is life
beyond this pain
and there is hope
waiting for the dawn.

loving you
feels like
speeding down the highway
with the top down
singing along to the radio
at the top of our lungs

our mistakes
are
our greatest
teachers

regret is a useless thing.
it does not change the past
it only causes us
to feel pain
because of it

so let go of your regret
unchain your soul
unfurl your wings
the new day has come
and it is time to be free.

do not be afraid
to love yourself

you of all people
deserve it

the world may seem
to have gone berserk
but do not forget
to seek
your inner peace

contentment.

that's what i feel
as you run
your fingers
through my hair.

contentment.

cherish the people
who introduce you
to new places
new people
and new experiences

with the guiding hand
of a loving god
to hold you

what do you have
to be afraid of?

the answers to all things
will eventually come
we need not distress
over the questions of life
we need only live it
and learn to be at peace.

it is important
to keep singing
even though the dark times

do not lose your joy
for it is the
most powerful thing
you have.

your inner joy
cannot be taken from you
by anyone else

you have to surrender it
willingly
and choose to let it die

do not do so.
hold on
to your inner joy
and let it nourish you.

be strong
even when it's not
easy

for when it's most difficult
is when it means the most
to be strong

be grateful for when life
gets hard

for it teaches you
perseverance
and gives you
the ability
to stay strong
through even
the darkest of times

our pain, our suffering
it will all fade away

Chapter Three

The Light

when i was at my lowest point
broken and destitute
you reached down to me
and gave me love

you never know
what you have
until it's gone

never forget
that life
is not meant
to be a repetition
of the same day
over and over again

change something today
in some small way

in the sweeping strings
and uplifting piano
hope stirs my soul
and leaves love
where anxiety once was

dear one,
you are my definition
of perfect

stand still.
collect your thoughts.
let the rain wash down your
face.

find your peace.
here.

ripped jeans
burgundy sweaters
rings on

it's going to be
a good day

you may feel down

but remember
the only direction
that matters in life
is onward

i imagine once more
our silhouettes against the
sunset
at the edge of the ocean
the waves crashing on the
shore

i imagine once more
a moment so perfect
it haunts me to this day

when you have yourself
you lack nothing

every breath
i breathe
is yours

we spent a week in the woods
together
just hiking and adventuring
and when we returned
to the city
with dirt on our faces
and smelling of smoke
we stopped for coffee
and though everybody
looked at us funny
we didn't care
we just laughed it off

because
when it's just you and me
nothing else matters
no, nothing at all.

any day
spent with you
is a day
spent well.

sing a song
for the rain
harmonize
with the snow
be one
with nature

take me back
to that one night
where everything
just felt
so simple

it was just
you and i
and nothing else
mattered
in the whole world

be with someone
who lights up
your life

as you left
i whispered
"i love you"
hoping the gentle breeze
would carry it
from my heart
to yours

don't be ashamed
of feeling pain

life hurts
and that
is just part
of being alive

you
are a beautiful flower
just waiting
to bloom

we spent the whole night
talking
and before i knew it
the sun was up again
and it was time
to say goodbye

i find my peace
in you

Chapter Four

Forever

dear one,
we have travelled
this road
together
all these years
and i don't want it to end
but i fear
that it must.

dear one,
you are everything
that is wonderful
in this world

there is nothing
in the world
like exploring
with you.

you are my favorite wanderer.

you would not look
at the knife
that cut you
expecting it
to heal you

so do not look
at the people
who hurt you
expecting them
to heal you

we have only two choices
in this life

to live a life
of absolute freedom
taking everything
as it comes

or a life
of absolute enslavement
to routines and patterns

i know which one
i want.

you poured gasoline
on my heart
and threw a lit match
onto it
without a care

and then have the
sheer audacity
to complain
that i burn
too brightly

never be afraid to cry.

there is nothing like
letting out
your every emotion
to a sad song
or a sad movie

just let yourself feel
and let your heart be cleansed
by your tears
as your body
is cleansed by the rain.

i am forever in awe
of the beauty
of this world

we were meant
for each other

two broken souls
drifting through life
waiting for the stars to align
and bring us together

she said she was okay
but her eyes screamed
of pain unbearable
and love unrequited

dear one,
i would follow you
through deepest darkness
and barren desert

i would follow you
through heartbreak
and sorrow

i would follow you
wherever you lead me

there is nothing
in the world
like the feeling
of trusting someone
with your whole heart,
mind, and soul.

the problem with you leaving
is that you
were the only one
who ever truly
understood me

maybe it's not love
but it'll do
for the night

you are more
than your mistakes

you will move on
you will keep living
you will forget

do not be afraid
for even the darkness nights
have an end.

this morning
i woke up
feeling
for the first time
in a long time
that i could live
without you
and everything
would be okay

i want to live
in a world
where everyone
has equal rights
and everyone's voice
counts
for the same.

rome
was not built
in a day

you
cannot heal
your heart
in a day

but do not worry
time will pass
and you will heal.

you and i, my darling
i promise you this
i promise you forever
and every forever
after that

my all, my everything
my eternity
everything i am
is yours
now and forever.

THE END.

About This Book

"Dear One" is a poetry collection about love, heartbreak, longing, life, and healing. It is a breathtaking and beautiful journey through struggle and adventure.

Made in the USA
Lexington, KY
28 March 2018